Shaquille O'Neal

SPORTS REPORTS

Shaquille O'Neal

Star Center

Glen Macnow

Enslow Publishers, Inc.

44 Fadem Road   PO Box 38
Box 699   Aldershot
Springfield, NJ 07081   Hants GU12 6BP
USA   UK

Dedication

Dedicated to Professor Timothy Cohane,
who loved to write and knew how to teach it

Library of Congress Cataloging-in-Publication Data

Macnow, Glen.
    Shaquille O'Neal : star center / Glen Macnow.
      p. cm.—(Sports Reports)
    Includes bibliographical references (p.) and index.
    Summary: Relates the basketball career of the center for the Orlando
Magic who has also written books, recorded a rap album, and starred
in a movie.
    ISBN 0-89490-656-9
    1. O'Neal, Shaquille—Juvenile Literature. 2. Basketball players—United
States—Biography—Juvenile Literature. [1. O'Neal, Shaquille. 2. Basketball
players. 3. Afro-Americans—Biography.]
    I. Title. II. Series.
GV884.054M33 1996
796.323'092—dc20
[B]   96-3425
                                            CIP
                                            AC

Printed in the United States of America

10 9 8 7 6 5 4 3 2 1

Photo Credits: NBA Photos, pp. 9, 11, 14, 21, 30, 40, 43, 51, 55, 61, 67, 73, 75,
80, 89, 91.

Cover Illustration: AP/Wide World

Contents

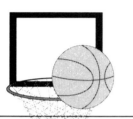

Chapter 1

Shaq Attack

The moment was brief. It lasted just seconds. It was not on television. There was no instant replay. The moment came at midcourt of Chicago's United Center on May 17, 1995, shortly after 11 P.M. More than twenty-one thousand fans crammed the arena that night, but, to most, the moment was just a blur.

The moment was a private embrace between two of the greatest talents ever to play basketball—Shaquille O'Neal and Michael Jordan. O'Neal's team, the Orlando Magic, had just beaten Jordan's club, the Chicago Bulls. In doing so, the Magic had knocked the Bulls out of the playoffs. O'Neal and his teammates would go on to play in the 1995 National Basketball Association finals. Jordan would go home.

"Now, you are the man," Jordan told O'Neal as they hugged. "Now, the future belongs to you." [1]

It was just a handful of words, but the meaning could fill that arena. There is no question that Michael Jordan was "the man" in the NBA. He was basketball's top star of the past decade—perhaps the top star of its history. In those few words and that quick hug, Jordan told O'Neal that, from now on, Shaq would be the sport's top star. The king was handing his throne to the crown prince. Shaq saw it another way. If Jordan was Superman, he said, he was just Superboy.

O'Neal had scored 32 points against the Bulls that night and pulled down 20 rebounds. He had forced three Bulls centers into foul trouble. Once, he slam-dunked the ball through the rim so hard that it bounced off of Luc Longley's head, causing the embarrassed Bulls center to tumble to the floor.

Still, the gracious words from Jordan caught O'Neal off guard. After the moment, the Magic's star center was humble—not his usual style. He told people that he still kept Jordan's autograph in a frame at his home.

"I'm just happy to have my name mentioned in the same breath as Michael Jordan," he told reporters. "Michael has already accomplished things I am just dreaming of doing." [2] Well, that is true. Jordan

Shaq drops one in.

won seven NBA scoring titles, to Shaq's one. Jordan has three NBA titles and three Most Valuable Player Awards. Shaq has yet to win either. He and the Magic would go on to lose the 1995 NBA finals against the Houston Rockets. But O'Neal is basketball's future. As the NBA enters the twenty-first century, there is little question that Shaquille Rashaun O'Neal is its star attraction—just as Jordan was the star attraction in recent years.

Everything about O'Neal is big. Big body. Big smile. Big future. His hands are so large—eleven inches long—that he can palm a basketball as if it were a grapefruit. His feet are so big—size 21EEE—that it would take a half gallon of water to fill one of his high tops. He looks strong enough to pluck tree trunks from the ground like flower stems. The Magic's general manager, Pat Williams, calls Shaq, "a Paul Bunyan in sneakers. He's a giant in every way."[3]

Since bursting into the NBA as a twenty-year-old in 1992, Shaq has been one tough giant. He plays center, the position reserved for seven-footers such as Hakeem Olajuwon, Patrick Ewing, and David Robinson. Shaq is tall (seven feet one inch) and also wide (305 pounds). He is all muscle. His style is not one of speed and sneaky moves, it is one of power and monster dunks. And he can jump. With a running

Shaquille O'Neal is the big man of the Orlando Magic. At seven feet one inch and three hundred pounds, he is a fearsome opponent.

start, Shaq can touch a spot on the backboard three feet above the rim.

One of the most famous plays of Shaq's young career shows his raw force. Playing against the Phoenix Suns in his rookie season, O'Neal slammed a walloping dunk over the head of Cedric Ceballos. On his way down, Shaq grabbed onto the rim. The force and weight caused the backboard to crash to the ground. At first, fans sat in shocked silence; then they gave Shaq a standing ovation. That season, O'Neal became the first rookie to start an NBA All-Star Game since Michael Jordan in 1985. Even though he was just the age of most college juniors, he finished the season second in the NBA in blocked shots, second in rebounds, fourth in field-goal percentage, and eighth in scoring. Not surprisingly, he was an overwhelming choice for Rookie of the Year.

From there, things have just gone up. In his second season, Shaq finished second in the league in scoring—just a half-point per game behind David Robinson of the San Antonio Spurs. He led the Magic to a 50–32 record, and the team made the playoffs for the first time in its five-year history.

"He's certainly one of the greatest players to come along in a long, long time," Golden State Warriors coach Don Nelson said that season. "If he stays around long enough, he'll be rated right up there with Bill Russell and Wilt Chamberlain and Wes Unseld and some of the other great centers that we've had."[4]

By his third NBA season, Shaq had earned a spot among basketball's premier players—worthy of the praise Jordan gave him. He won his first scoring title, averaging 29.3 points per game. He led the Magic past the Bulls, Boston Celtics, and Indiana Pacers, and into the NBA Finals.

Orlando, however, was no match for the Houston Rockets and their great center, Hakeem Olajuwon. The Rockets swept the series, four games to none. But even in losing, Shaq and his all-star teammate Anfernee "Penny" Hardaway gave warning that they have moved to the top of the NBA.

"Penny and I are the Magic Johnson and Kareem Abdul-Jabbar of the '90s," Shaq has boasted.[5] Ouch. Johnson and Abdul-Jabbar won five NBA titles in nine seasons.

But if O'Neal compares himself with other great NBA players, he will see that titles sometimes take time. Jordan didn't earn a championship ring until his seventh season. Olajuwon played ten years before he won one. As long as O'Neal and Hardaway stay healthy, Orlando should win—and win more than once.

More than anything, Shaquille O'Neal knows

Using his size and strength, Shaq stretches past the Indiana Pacers and places the ball in the net.

how to have fun. He is a man, but his pleasures are those of a big kid. He loves movies, especially those with gangsters or kung fu fighters. He loves pizza, orange soda, and rap music. He plays CDs so loud that neighbors in his Orlando neighborhood complain about the noise.

He owns so many video games that his home looks like an arcade. Sometimes, he cracks up his teammates by break dancing. He'll spin his huge body around the floor like a top.

Shaq doesn't just entertain teammates and basketball fans. His two rap albums have gone to the top of the charts. He co-starred in a movie, *Blue Chips*, and drew rave reviews for his performance. Recently, he opened a restaurant in Orlando where the specialty is double cheeseburgers and the decor is broken backboards. All of that has combined to make the man one of America's most popular entertainers.

The toys and the games and the music merely occupy his idle time. Shaq is consumed by a vision of guiding the Magic to an NBA championship and becoming the best player in the league. Those who see Shaq as a fun-loving guy don't see the entire story. They don't see the hours upon hours he devotes to training and practice. They don't see the scratches and bruises that cover his body. Playing the rough-and-tumble style Shaq plays means banging bodies with other three-hundred-pound men night after night. It all takes a toll.

When he needs to escape from it all, O'Neal jumps into one of his many cars (he has license plates reading "Shaq Attack" and "Shaqnificant") and just starts driving. His cars, with their added leg room and fabulous sound systems, are the only place he can be alone. Sometimes he doesn't know where he's headed, he just drives until his worries and tension are gone. Then he returns home.

There is also a gentle side to this rim-rattling Goliath. Every Thanksgiving he takes time to visit a homeless shelter. He'll pass out food and sit down to talk with the homeless people. At the end of the night, he'll write out a check to cover hundreds of people's meals.

One Christmas, O'Neal made three trips to a local toy store to pick out presents. He bought enough to fill up three trucks, and then he personally delivered the toys to one hundred fifty poor children. Most of them just stared at the seven-foot Santa Claus.

Young people are important to Shaq. He can identify with their troubles because he was once a troubled teen himself. Before he found basketball, Shaq was, in his own words, a wise guy. At the time, he was a six-foot-six thirteen-year-old who couldn't dunk a basketball or get out of the way of his own feet. He kept getting into fist fights, and he was constantly in trouble at school.

Shaq's parents worked hard to straighten him out. Even when Shaq was a gangly teen, his father promised him that if he worked hard enough—and stayed out of trouble—he would be the best basketball player in the world.

"If more kids had my upbringing there would be a lot less trouble," Shaq said. "Everything my dad ever said came true. Everything. He told me I would be a great basketball player and play on national television and be well-known. When I started to get good, I thought, 'Wow. This man knows what he's talking about. I'd better pay attention.'"[6]

Even now, as an adult, O'Neal stands at attention when his father, a retired Army sergeant, starts talking. He wears a small, gold earring only because his father says that it's okay.

Hard work and dedication have put Shaq at the top of his sport, as have size and natural ability. So, too, has listening to his parents. That's where his story starts.

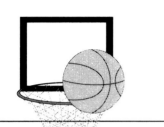

Chapter 2

Moving Around

Shaquille was born on March 6, 1972, in Newark, New Jersey. His mom, Lucille O'Neal Harrison, came up with Shaquille as the name for her first born. She gave him a middle name, too: Rashaun. Shaquille Rashaun is Muslim. It means "little warrior." Twenty years later, the warrior part would fit just right. But little?

O'Neal's early years were tough. Later, he would say that his poverty as a young child would make him enjoy his success as an adult that much more. When Shaq was a baby, his father Joseph Toney abandoned the family and ended up in jail. Shaq's mom worked two jobs to get by, and young Shaquille spent his days with aunts and uncles. For a while, mother and son needed food stamps to help them get by.[1]

When he grew up, Shaq wrote a rap song about Joseph Toney. It was an angry song. The message was that young men should not father babies that they cannot support. "What's going on is terrible, the way fathers desert families, and the way young girls have babies and the boy cuts out," Shaq said. "Something's got to be done about it. If I can help even one person out of 10, or out of 100, that's good."[2]

When Shaquille was two years old, his mom met and married a man named Phillip Harrison. He was a big—six feet five and 250 pounds—and loving man. He adopted Shaquille as his own son. Phillip and Lucille had three other children, giving Shaq two sisters and one brother.

To improve life for his family, Phillip Harrison joined the army. It meant a good paycheck and good schools for the kids, but it also meant moving almost every year. In less than ten years, the family moved to army bases in New Jersey, Germany, New Jersey again, Georgia, Germany again, and then Texas. This was tough for Shaquille. He didn't like adjusting to new schools and trying to make new friends, and he was uncomfortable with his size. By age eleven, Shaq was already more than six feet tall. Kids teased him by calling him "Bigfoot." Shaq slouched to look more average sized, but, of course, it didn't work.

Because he was unhappy, Shaq started hanging with a tough group of kids. He got into fist fights nearly every day. Once, he got caught setting off a fire alarm in school. He was brought to the military police office, and the police called his father. Phillip Harrison came and, in front of the police, spanked Shaq with a ping-pong paddle.

Shaq says his father hit him because he loved him. Mr. Harrison was trying to straighten out the angry young boy. "I was a real jerk, but I thought I was cool," Shaquille now says. "I'd beat people up, hit teachers, spit on people, break into cars and take tapes."[3] Finally, Shaq realized that the road he was taking would lead him to disaster. He asked his dad to help him find a new path—one that would lead to success.

So Shaq's father introduced him to basketball. Phillip Harrison knew that the big, strong youngster could star at the sport, but Shaq had other ideas. He wanted to be a break dancer. His plan was to become a professional dancer on television and in the theater, so he practiced until he could do head spins and slither along the ground. But he also kept growing. By age thirteen, Shaq was six feet six inches tall, too big to spin on his head. Break dancing was out, and suddenly, basketball looked a lot better.[4]

Even from above, Shaq's feet look enormous. He was already wearing a size seventeen when he was just thirteen years old.

He was now at the age where kids look for role models. He liked Michael Jordan and Magic Johnson. Then, one day, he realized he didn't have to search that far. "My parents were my role models," he said. "All I had to do was pattern myself after them."

At this time, Shaq and his family were living on an army base in Germany. The tall teen spent his free time trying to improve his basketball skills. He was frustrated that he couldn't jump high enough to dunk the ball. Plus, he couldn't get very good coaching in Germany. Then, one day, Shaq heard that Dale Brown, the head coach at Louisiana State University, was visiting the army base to hold some basketball workshops for the soldiers. Shaq, even though he was six years younger than the soldiers, snuck in and sat in the first row as Brown spoke.

At the end of the day, Shaq walked up to Brown and asked if the coach knew exercises to help him jump higher.

Brown looked up at the tall youngster and asked: "Soldier, how big are your feet?"

"Size 17, sir," O'Neal said.

"And how old are you, soldier?" Brown asked.

"Oh, sir, I'm not enlisted. I'm 13."

Without missing a beat, Coach Brown said: "Son, where can I find your father?"[5]

In the sauna, it turned out. And Coach Brown, in a business suit, went right into that sauna. Dripping sweat, he walked up to Mr. Harrison and asked if maybe he could keep an eye on Shaquille so that, perhaps, the youngster could someday play for him in college. Shaq's dad listened as the coach talked about basketball, but after a minute, Harrison stuck his own large hand against Brown's chest and spoke.

He said that basketball was fine, but he was more concerned with his son's education. There are plenty of black people who are laborers and army sergeants and assistant coaches, Mr. Harrison said, but he wanted his son to become a manager or general or head coach. If Coach Brown could help him reach those goals, they could work together.[6]

Coach Brown agreed, and the two men stayed in touch. When Shaq was fifteen, his father was transferred to Fort Sam Houston in San Antonio, Texas. It was another move, which meant another adjustment for the youngster. But this time it wasn't as tough. Shaq—by now six feet eight inches—had become comfortable with his giant size. In fact, he was proud of it. And his skill at basketball made him happier to be around other people. He made new friends quickly. In fact, he headed a silly group called the Knuckle-head Club. Members would salute each other by touching their knuckles to their foreheads.

His other hobbies were rap singing and video games. Once, without telling his parents, Shaq even tried the dangerous sport of bungee jumping. Instead of tying the rubber cord to his ankle, as most bungee jumpers do, Shaq tied it to his waist before diving off a high bridge.

Mostly, though, his time was spent on schoolwork and basketball. Now able to dunk the ball, he practiced new techniques and jumps by the hour. Shaq's parents, however, told him that no matter how good he got at basketball, he wouldn't go far in life without a good education.

Shaq's high school was the Robert Cole School. Most of the kids there were the children of military officers at Fort Sam Houston. There were always a lot of good athletes, so Shaq didn't know how he would do on the Cougars basketball team.

No need to worry. Cole's coach, Dave Madura, took one look at the giant fifteen-year-old and saw a player around whom he could build. Shaq's dad, a good high school player in his day, had taught the boy solid fundamentals. Coach Madura taught him how to deal with the double- and triple-teaming he was sure to face. While other teens were out partying, Shaq was in the gym working on his dunks and jump shots.

In Shaq's junior year, the Cougars won 32 of 33

games. The team was considered the best in the state going into the Texas state playoffs, but in the first two minutes of the playoff game Shaq got four fouls. He had to sit and watch, and his teammates could not stay in the game without him. It was a disappointment—but one from which he learned.

The next season, Shaquille and his team were even better. They won all 36 games, including the Texas state championship. Shaq had grown to seven feet tall and weighed 245 pounds. He could run like a deer. Writers started calling him Shaquille "The Real Deal" O'Neal. His statistics backed the name up: He averaged 32.1 points, 22 rebounds, and 8 blocked shots per game. Some believed he was the best player in Texas high school history.

That spring, Shaq made his national television debut. He played in the McDonalds All-American game, a contest of the country's best high school players. In one play, seen coast to coast, he blocked a shot on defense, grabbed the loose ball, and dribbled the length of the court. No one could stop him. He finished off with a power-slamming dunk. It was a terrific play for a pro, an incredible feat for a high school kid.

That kind of incredible play prompted college coaches to start hanging around Cole High's gym. All of them wanted Shaq to attend their school, to star for their program. But Shaq had stayed in touch with Coach Brown over the years. There was only one college that interested him and his family—Louisiana State University.

Shaquille eagerly signed up to attend LSU. The experts who follow college basketball said that Coach Brown had landed America's best young player. One of those experts, talent scout Bob Gibbons, predicted that Shaq would grow up to be better than the great Hakeem Olajuwon.[7]

It was a lot of pressure for a seventeen-year-old boy to face, but Shaq was ready. Mentally, his parents had taught him to deal with tough situations. Physically, Shaq just kept growing and growing. He worked a job carrying bricks at a construction site the summer before college and gained fifty pounds. By the time he arrived on LSU's campus in the fall of 1989, O'Neal was seven feet one inch tall and weighed 290 pounds.

He was ready to hit college basketball by storm.

Chapter 3

LSU Tiger

In fact, Shaquille O'Neal hit Louisiana State University the same day as a giant storm. On his first day on campus, a violent tornado blew through the city of Baton Rouge, where LSU is located. The tornado was an omen of Shaq's sensational but stormy career as an LSU Tiger.

Like any new college student, Shaq had a lot to adjust to. He was seventeen years old and living away from his parents for the first time. He had to make his own rules and be responsible for his actions. He had to live by his own decisions. But Shaq was lucky; his parents had taught him well. He was more mature and prepared for college than most first-year students.

Even a good upbringing could not prepare Shaq

for the attention he got on the basketball court. Shaq had arrived on campus as headline news—the country's best and biggest high school recruit.

LSU students crowded into the gym to watch him practice. In preseason games, fans at other colleges packed arenas to cheer—or boo—the latest sensation. Shaq had no privacy. Newspapers wrote about what he ate for breakfast. Television stations filmed him walking to the college library.

Shaq felt as if all eyes were focused on him, and it made him nervous. Remember, he was just seventeen years old.

That nervousness showed in his first college game. Trying as hard as he could—perhaps too hard—Shaq was whistled for three fouls in the game's first seven minutes. He finished with just 10 points before fouling out.

LSU Coach Dale Brown quickly saw what was happening. His prize recruit was feeling too much pressure, so Brown decided to lighten the load. Three games into the season, he took Shaq out of the starting lineup. "He's going to be a great, great, great player," Coach Brown said. "But he needs time. Let's not rush him."[1]

The coach gave Shaq a new job. No longer would Shaq be a starting center that other teams could triple-team. Instead, he became the first substitute to come off the bench each game. This way, other teams couldn't plan their strategy around guarding him. Brown was careful to tell Shaq that he wasn't being punished. Instead, the move was designed to improve his skills.

Besides, the coach argued, Shaq wasn't the only talented player at Louisiana State. Going into the 1989–90 season, the Tigers were ranked as the country's second best team. Many college basketball experts believed LSU might win that season's NCAA Tournament, which would make it the national champion.

And why not? The team had finished 20–12 the season before. It already had All-American guard Chris Jackson, who had averaged more than 30 points per game in 1988–89, and it had center Stanley Roberts. Like Shaq, Roberts stood more than seven feet tall and weighed 290 pounds. Adding Shaq to this mix made LSU appear unbeatable.

"Their big guys scare me to death," Vanderbilt University coach Eddie Fogler said at the start of the season. "First Roberts and now this new kid? O'Neal will be great. How about a seven-feet-one guy who can run like a five-feet-eleven guy? He'll be tremendous."[2]

Shaq was tremendous, or, at least, pretty close to it. As a freshman he averaged nearly 14 points

Shaq proved to be one of the best blockers in NCAA history. He broke many records at LSU.

and 12 rebounds per game. Under Coach Brown's strategy of bringing him off the bench, Shaq improved week to week. More than anything, he was a defensive star. He averaged more than three blocked shots per game. Opposing players knew better than to try taking shots near the LSU basket. That was Shaq's territory. Those foolish enough to try often got the ball swatted back in their face.

"Most of the time I try to keep the ball in play," Shaq said. "But sometimes, I still try to kill it to let them know, 'Don't bring it in here again.'"[3]

Shaq didn't have to try hard to scare the other guys. He just did it. In one game, University of North Carolina center Eric Montross got between Shaq and a slam dunk. Big mistake. Montross went away with a six-stitch gash over his eye. Another time, Indiana's Damon Bailey tried to block Shaq's way to the basket.

O'Neal went over the six-foot-seven Bailey and slammed the ball through the hoop. On his way down, Shaq grabbed the rim and pulled it right off the backboard. That was the first time in his life that Shaq tore down the basket. It certainly wouldn't be the last.

As impressive as Shaq's first college season was, the Tigers were a disappointment. Starting center Stanley Roberts ballooned up to 320 pounds and stopped being a productive player. By the end of the year, Roberts was thrown off the team because of bad grades. Guard Chris Jackson was still brilliant, but he and Shaq couldn't do it alone. At season's end, LSU was ranked nineteenth in the nation. Not bad, but not as good as people had expected.

The news got worse after the season ended. Roberts quit school and went to Spain to play pro basketball. Jackson, too, left LSU. He was drafted by the NBA's Denver Nuggets with the third overall pick.

Those two departures left Shaq alone as the Tigers only star player. Coming back for his sophomore season, he was surrounded by college newcomers and players who had spent the previous year sitting on LSU's bench. If the pressure put on Shaq had been large a year ago, it was now gigantic.

But over that year Shaq had grown—not so much in size, but in his maturity. He was now ready to be the center of attention. He was working hard, both in and out of the classroom. The youngster who had been a class clown a few years back was now cracking the books. He kept a B average, even while taking some tough business courses. In basketball practice, he spent hours working on the basics. One day he vowed not to leave the gym until he hit twenty-five free throws in a row. It took three hours, but he finally did it.

Shaq also dedicated himself to growing stronger. Ed Ortega, the Tigers' strength and conditioning coach, said O'Neal would work so hard in the weight room that Ortega would see the young man rolling on the ground in pain.[4] Eventually, the weight lifting machines at LSU had to be altered to hold his massive arms.

"I don't have any trouble working out on my own and pushing myself," O'Neal said. "I just say to myself I want to be the best, I want to sign the biggest NBA contract. I just work on things I have to work on."[5]

Away from schoolwork and basketball, there was another side to Shaq. There still is. He has always liked loud music, especially rap. He loves to dance, sometimes flopping on the floor to imitate the Three Stooges. He is also a practical joker. One time he tricked his teammates into entering a bathroom at the LSU Athletic Center and then locked them all in.

On the court, however, he has always been all business. As a sophomore, O'Neal grew from being a very good player into the best college player in the country. He averaged 27.6 points and 14.7

rebounds per game and won the Adolph Rupp Award as the nation's player of the year.

Shaq's best game came against Arkansas State University in December 1990. Early on, however, Shaq had trouble. He missed four straight shots in the game's first five minutes. Coach Brown pulled him from the lineup and sent him to the bench to think. O'Neal was unhappy watching, and he liked it less when his teammates fell behind without him.

After a few minutes, Brown called a timeout and walked over to O'Neal on the bench.

"Shaq, you're playing weak," said the coach. "Too many dumb shots."

"You're right," said O'Neal.

"I want you to go back into the game and take over."[6]

Shaq did just that. He scored sixteen points in the first half and an amazing thirty-seven in the second half. The 53 points broke the school record held by former teammate Chris Jackson. Shaq also grabbed 19 rebounds and blocked 5 shots.

Shaq quickly became recognized as college basketball's best player. His highlights made the nightly sports shows. Against the University of Arizona, he stole the ball and dunked it with ten seconds left to give LSU an 84–82 win. Against

Georgia Tech, he collided with the rim so hard that he turned the backboard halfway around.

Surprisingly, the Tigers were one of the country's best college teams in 1990–91. It was a surprise because O'Neal was their only great player. Single-handedly, the sophomore center pushed LSU into the NCAA Tournament.

But once again, the year ended in disappointment. Late in the season, Shaq suffered a small break in a leg bone. It wasn't a serious injury, but it kept him out of five important games. He came back

FACT

Highlights of Shaquille O'Neal's college career:

- National Player of the Year, 1991
- Consensus first-team All America in 1991 and 1992
- Southeastern Conference (SEC) Athlete of the Year, 1991
- National leader in rebounding (14.7 average), 1991
- Led SEC in rebounding, field-goal percentage, and blocked shots and was second in scoring, 1992
- First Player to lead the SEC in rebounding three consecutive seasons since Auburn's Charles Barkley, 1982–84
- Most Valuable Player on SEC Coaches Defensive Team, 1991–1992

in time for the NCAA Tournament. Although he scored 27 points, LSU lost to the University of Connecticut, 79–62. The Tigers finished the season with 20 wins and 10 losses.

As soon as the season ended, there was talk of whether O'Neal would quit school and turn pro, as teammates Jackson and Roberts had the year before. He was just nineteen years old, but he could make as much as $50 million by joining the NBA.

The money was tempting, but Shaq and his parents decided he should stay at LSU. For one, he enjoyed the campus life. And the NBA wasn't going anywhere. He could turn pro later on.

"Most players come out because their family has money problems," said O'Neal. "My family is doing real fine. We don't have any problems. So I want to stay in school and get my degree. I can't wait until next season."[7]

Chapter 4

College Star

By the start of his third year in college, Shaquille O'Neal was a national celebrity. He was already one of those players, like Magic and Michael, who doesn't need a last name for identification.

Shaq was enough.

Wherever the LSU Tigers traveled, the cameras focused on O'Neal. Fans swarmed him. Reporters tugged at him for interviews. One Louisiana couple even named their first child Shaquille O'Neal Long. When Shaq heard about that, he drove his Ford Explorer to their house to take pictures with the baby.

"I think they were a little shocked when I showed up at the door," O'Neal said. "But the father told me, 'I knew you'd come.'"[1]

Life as a student was fun for Shaq. He was a prankster, imitating his head coach and setting off fireworks in a teammate's dorm room. He was a party animal, loving double cheeseburgers and gangster movies. He was a part-time disk jockey, spinning rap records on the two turntables at his apartment.

O'Neal would parade around the LSU campus in a black baseball cap with messages reading "Shaqnificent" or "The Real Deal." He was not trying to be smug. He was just being himself—a fun-loving, giant-sized youngster.

"I'm a kid and that's why I like kids," O'Neal said. "I want to stay a kid for as long as possible. My mom, she treats me like a baby. She worries about me all the time. That's cool."[2]

On the basketball court, of course, Shaq was anything but a kid. He was a man among boys. He wasn't just a great college player at age nineteen. He was a great player—period. Boston Celtics star Larry Bird said that the two best basketball players in the world were Michael Jordan and Shaquille O'Neal. University of Kentucky coach Rick Pitino compared O'Neal to Wilt Chamberlain and Bill Russell, perhaps the two best centers ever.

Not many people argued. Once the 1991–92 season began, Shaq was more dominant than ever. In a nationally televised game in December, he single-handedly destroyed Arizona, then the Number 2-ranked team. Arizona boasted a front line that measured six feet eleven, six feet eleven, and seven feet. Shaq broke through them like a bulldozer. He scored 29 points, grabbed 14 rebounds, and blocked 6 shots.

In another game against Florida, Shaq slam-dunked the ball 11 times. He pushed one dunk through the net so violently that he bent the rim. It had to be replaced. After the game, which LSU won, O'Neal led teammates in a dance he called the "Dunk Mob Epsilon," swaying his hips and rubbing his head.

Shaq enjoyed playing with his Tiger teammates. There was no jealousy, because Shaq did not act big-headed around them. "A lot of superstars breathe life out of a team," Coach Brown said. "Very few breathe life into a team. Shaq does. He does it with great dignity. He has no ego."[3]

Games at LSU's Maravich Center became a three-ring circus during the 1991–92 season. Before each contest, a real Bengal tiger ran around the court on a leash. Then, a student dressed in a tiger costume slid down a rope to midcourt. Indoor fireworks greeted the team as it took the floor for warmups, and when the smoke finally cleared,

Despite his size, Shaq is quick. When he gets in front of the net, players stand back.

O'Neal took over and did everything short of bringing down the backboard.

It all should have been great for O'Neal. His statistics were impressive—24.1 points, 14 rebounds, and 5.2 blocked shots per game. And the Tigers were a good team, winning 21 games and losing just 10.

But basketball—at least at the college level—was becoming a chore. Because Shaq was the only talented player on his team, opponents were ganging up on him. Each time he touched the ball, three or four players would hack him and elbows would fly in his face. Shaq had no room to use his size and strength.

Coach Brown and Shaq's dad complained that the referees were letting opponents get away with fouling Shaq. "The other guys are pushing him in the back, hitting him in the crotch," said Sgt. Harrison. "They're going to wind up hurting him out there. Why won't the officials do something? I guess that's because it's hard to treat someone 7-feet-1 and 294 pounds as an underdog."[4]

The problem came to a head in a late-season game against the University of Tennessee Volunteers. Throughout the game, Tennessee players grabbed Shaq, jostled him, and fouled him. Still, the Tigers led by twenty-two points with ten minutes to go. Then, Shaq launched himself upward for still another monster slam, but he never reached the rim. The Volunteers' Carlus Groves grabbed him around the waist, hauled him backward, and wrestled him to the floor.

O'Neal had taken enough. He lost his cool. He threw an elbow at Groves, prompting a bench-clearing brawl. The referees ejected five players from each team—most importantly Shaq. With the big man out of the game, Tennessee whittled twelve points off the LSU lead before falling, 99–89.

O'Neal was steaming afterward. He believed that he had been punished for protecting himself. Then, things got worse. The NCAA, a body that sets rules for college sports, suspended Shaq for the next game. That happened to be a crucial contest against the University of Kentucky. Without Shaq, the Tigers lost badly.

After the loss, O'Neal, his dad, and Coach Brown sat down to talk. They agreed that Shaq had nothing left to prove in college basketball. They agreed that his game was being strangled by opponents' hacks and fouls. They agreed that, without protection from the refs, Shaq might get hurt playing for LSU. He had one more year to play ball for the Tigers, but it no longer seemed worth it.

"I'm recommending to Shaquille's parents that

Shaq is usually a good sport, but like everyone else, he has bad days, too.

he turns pro," Coach Brown said. "I do not want to see this young man blatantly fouled and hurt. If he's going to get hurt and people are going to intentionally foul him, he needs to go get money."[5]

As much as Shaq had dreamed of staying in college until he graduated, he agreed the time had come to move on. He could take classes and graduate later. For now, if he was going to trade slam dunks and elbows, he didn't want to do it against college kids, but against NBA stars like Patrick Ewing, David Robinson, and Hakeem Olajuwon.

On March 21, 1992, LSU was eliminated by the University of Indiana, 89–79, in the second round

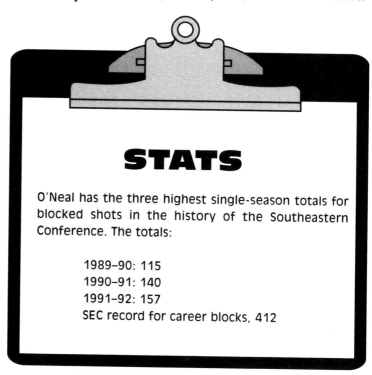

STATS

O'Neal has the three highest single-season totals for blocked shots in the history of the Southeastern Conference. The totals:

1989–90: 115
1990–91: 140
1991–92: 157
SEC record for career blocks, 412

of the NCAA Tournament. Shaq scored 36 points and added 12 rebounds and 5 blocks. It was an impressive way to close his college career.

Two weeks later, O'Neal made the official announcement. With his family by his side, Shaq said he would give up his senior season of basketball to enter the National Basketball Association. He promised his mother that he would keep working toward his degree in business administration during the off-season.

Dozens of reporters gathered to hear what Shaq had to say. "I'm not making this decision out of anger or frustration," he told them. "But everyone who saw the Tennessee game knows that an injustice was done. The main factor was if I go back to school next year, will I have fun? And this year, I didn't have that much fun. My Dad told me at a young age, if you're not having fun at what you're doing, it's time to do something else."[6]

O'Neal described himself as happy and sad at the same time. He said he would miss the students, the fans, and the players at Louisiana State. He promised to continue his college education, and he also promised to use the first money he made in pro basketball to buy his mother a big house and his father a new car.

He also announced other plans—adult plans.

With some of the millions of dollars he would now earn, O'Neal said he wanted to open a chain of big-men's clothing stores all over the country. "Real big-men stores," he said. "The ones I go in now, the clothes don't fit guys taller than 6-feet-4. That's no big man."[7]

O'Neal was definitely a big man. Bigger than even he knew. His decision to turn pro rocked the NBA. There was no question that he would be the first player taken in the 1992 draft of college players. Many coaches described him as the kind of player who comes along once every decade—if that often. His sculpted body reminded experts of Wilt Chamberlain. His long arms were like those of Bill Russell. He was as tall as Kareem Abdul-Jabbar and moved gracefully, like Bill Walton. All of those players were Hall-of-Famers. And Shaq's discipline and determination reminded some of David Robinson, the star center for the San Antonio Spurs.

Eleven NBA teams had a shot at drafting O'Neal. Those happened to be the eleven teams that failed to make the 1992 playoffs or, in other words, the eleven worst teams in the league. Under the NBA's system, ping-pong balls with each team's name were put into a barrel. Then, the balls were mixed up and one was picked out. That team would draft first. That team would certainly draft Shaq.

It meant that Shaq had no say in where he would

play in the NBA. In his heart, he wanted to play for the Los Angeles Lakers, but that seemed a longshot at best.

On May 17, 1992, officials of the eleven teams met in a television studio in Secaucus, New Jersey. Dallas Mavericks owner Donald Carter sat in a chair rubbing a small stone for good luck. Next to him sat Pat Williams, general manager of the Orlando Magic. Williams admired the stone, and Carter let him rub it.

The good luck charm worked—but not for the Dallas Mavericks. When the ping-pong ball was pulled from the barrel, it carried the name of the Orlando Magic. That team, which had the NBA's second-worst record the year before, won the chance to draft Shaquille O'Neal.

Chapter 5

Million-Dollar Center

By winning the 1992 draft lottery, Orlando hit the Shaqpot. There was no doubt that the Magic would choose center Shaquille Rashaun O'Neal as their first-round draft pick.

On lottery night, the people of Orlando celebrated. The club sold more than five hundred new season tickets in just two hours. T-shirts with O'Neal's face on them began appearing all over town. In humid central Florida, Shaq was as welcome as air conditioning.

And why not? The Magic had lost three of every four games it played the season before. In its three previous seasons, Orlando was a dreary 70–176. Now there was hope. Now there was someone to build around.

In his first comments after the draft, O'Neal was modest. He told reporters: "I'm not promising a championship my first year. Things take time. But I'll learn the ropes, get my feet wet and become a good player."[1]

First, of course, he had to sign a contract to play for Orlando. If Shaq was the biggest new name to hit the NBA in years, he would have to be paid that way. And he was, signing a contract worth $40 million over seven years. To come up with the money, the Magic had to redo the contracts of five players, waive one player, and trade another. But most fans agreed that the club still got a bargain.

With his first paycheck, Shaq bought his parents a new Mercedes, his sister a Mustang, and himself a Ford Bronco; but most of the money went into the bank. Wealth, he promised, would not change him. "I was rich in thought before I was ever a million-aire," O'Neal said. "When I signed my contract, I just told myself, 'Stay the same.'"[2]

The most important things, he said, were those he learned from his father: a strong work ethic, wisdom, and responsibility.

That doesn't mean Shaq couldn't have fun. Orlando is the home of Disney World, so after signing his contract, Shaq arrived in town wearing Mickey Mouse ears. The next day, he took some of his buddies on their first tour of the Magic Kingdom. All the kids visiting the park flocked to this seven-foot giant with their parents in tow. Shaq laughed through it all. He tried to check out a water-raft ride, but found there wasn't room for him on the raft. So Shaq let his friends climb on him and they rode Mt. Shaq down the course.

Shaq was coming into the National Basketball Association at an important time. Two of the league's top stars—Larry Bird and Magic Johnson—had just retired. Only Michael Jordan remained among the superstars who could sell tickets in every town. Shaquille O'Neal—strong, talented, and loaded with personality—was just what the NBA needed.

It didn't take long for him to make an impact. O'Neal's first NBA game was against the Miami Heat. He was matched up against Rony Seikely who, at six feet ten, was good, but no superstar. O'Neal played carefully, focusing on his defense. He played thirty-two minutes before fouling out, scoring 12 points and grabbing 18 rebounds.

From there, things just exploded. Two nights later, O'Neal out-rebounded the Washington Bullets' starting five by himself and scored 22 points. Against the Charlotte Hornets he scored 35 points in just three quarters. In the next game against

In his first week in the NBA, O'Neal exploded onto the court. Against the New Jersey Nets, the rookie scored 29 points.

Washington he scored 31 points, including two on a pile-driving dunk that came after he dribbled the length of the floor. Then, against the New Jersey Nets, he scored 29. He was so unstoppable that the Nets first-string center, Sam Bowie, and second-string center, Chris Dudley, both fouled out. Both just looked on as O'Neal squeezed the ball like a grapefruit, faked a pass, then scooped in a basket.

At the end of his first week in the NBA, Shaq was averaging 26 points and 16 rebounds per game. The Magic had won three of five games. He was named the league's Player of the Week, the first time that any rookie had done that in his first week in the pros. Indeed, Shaq went on to win the Player of the Month Award, the first time a rookie had done that entering the NBA.

"He's good for the league, but bad for opponents," said Sam Bowie. "When you're seven-feet tall, you're supposed to have some limitations, but I haven't seen any. He's something very scary. If every new guy is getting to be like that, I'd better sit down and watch for a while."[3]

The experts who follow the NBA tried to come up with a player they could compare to this hot rookie. Most of them agreed that you had to go back more than thirty years to find anyone who entered the league with the impact of Shaquille O'Neal.

That man was Wilt Chamberlain, also known as "The Big Dipper." Many basketball fans consider Chamberlain the best center ever in the game.

Wilt, like Shaq, left college early because he did not enjoy being triple-teamed. He played one season with the Harlem Globetrotters, then joined the Philadelphia Warriors in 1959. Like Shaq, he was a

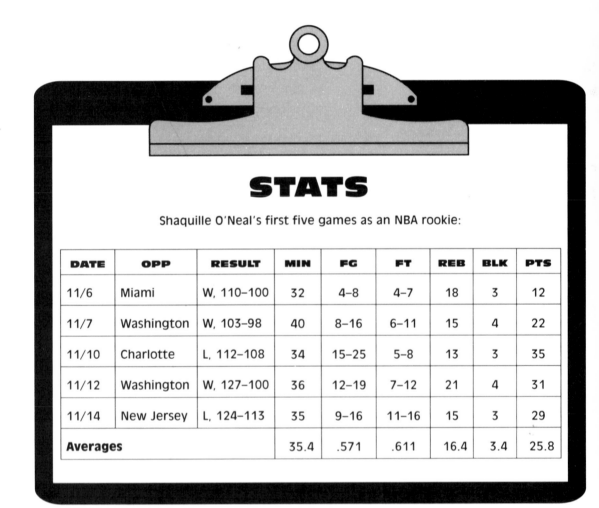

STATS

Shaquille O'Neal's first five games as an NBA rookie:

DATE	OPP	RESULT	MIN	FG	FT	REB	BLK	PTS
11/6	Miami	W, 110–100	32	4–8	4–7	18	3	12
11/7	Washington	W, 103–98	40	8–16	6–11	15	4	22
11/10	Charlotte	L, 112–108	34	15–25	5–8	13	3	35
11/12	Washington	W, 127–100	36	12–19	7–12	21	4	31
11/14	New Jersey	L, 124–113	35	9–16	11–16	15	3	29
Averages			35.4	.571	.611	16.4	3.4	25.8

giant—seven feet one inch tall and 285 pounds. Wilt might have been the strongest player ever. No one stopped him from going to the bucket, either for a basket or a rebound.

As a rookie, Chamberlain led the NBA in scoring and won the Most Valuable Player Award. Shaq would not go on to do that. But remember, Shaq was twenty years old as a rookie; Chamberlain was twenty-three.

The two men met that season. They were filming a sneaker commercial. Also in the ad were Bill Russell, Bill Walton, and Kareem-Abdul Jabbar, who were all Hall of Fame centers. The premise of the commercial was that the four retired players were welcoming O'Neal into their exclusive club.

Asked his opinion of Shaq, Chamberlain said, "I was impressed with the young man. I thought he had a lot of class, style, and enthusiasm. He's electrifying. He's a tremendous shot-blocker and he's extremely graceful."[4]

As his rookie season went on, O'Neal just kept getting better. During a nationally televised game in February 1993, he drove down the lane for a slam dunk. On the way down, he hung onto the rim. His three-hundred-pound body snapped a steel hook in the post that held up the backboard. The backboard crumpled to the ground. The game was delayed thirty-seven minutes while workmen put up a new basket, but the fans loved it.

Later that month, NBA fans voted Shaq to start in the NBA All-Star game in Salt Lake City. At twenty years old, he was the youngest All-Star ever. All of the All-Stars were given special rings before the game. Shaq took his off and gave it to his father. During the game, Shaq scored 14 points and

Though Shaq was a star from the beginning, he just wanted to be treated like one of the guys.

grabbed 7 rebounds. Afterward, all the older NBA players sat around talking about this new star.

Shaq's own teammates were also impressed. They looked up to him as the team star, but, as in college, Shaq just wanted to be one of the guys. He even formed a new version of the "Knucklehead Club," his old group from high school. When he and teammates Dennis Scott and Nick Anderson were introduced before the game, they would run onto the court pressing their knuckles to their foreheads.

By season's end, the Orlando Magic were the

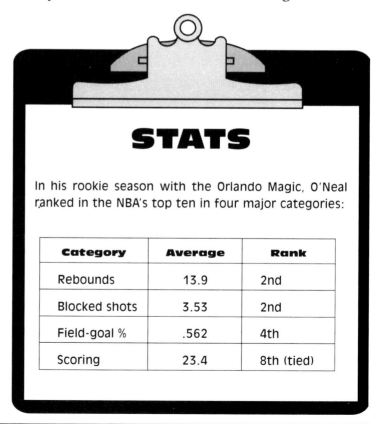

STATS

In his rookie season with the Orlando Magic, O'Neal ranked in the NBA's top ten in four major categories:

Category	Average	Rank
Rebounds	13.9	2nd
Blocked shots	3.53	2nd
Field-goal %	.562	4th
Scoring	23.4	8th (tied)

most-improved team in the NBA. They almost doubled their victory total from the previous year. No other team even came close. Of course, no other team had drafted rookie sensation Shaquille O'Neal.

O'Neal averaged 23.4 points, 13.9 rebounds, and 3.5 blocked shots per game, leading all rookies in each category. He also turned the Magic from one of the league's most unknown teams into one of its glamour teams. The Magic drew sellout crowds at almost every stop. Only Michael Jordan and the Chicago Bulls did better.

So no one was surprised when Shaq was named the NBA's Rookie of the Year after the season ended. The only surprise was that it wasn't unanimous. Shaq got ninety-six of the possible ninety-eight votes from a panel of sports writers and broadcasters. Charlotte Hornets center Alonzo Mourning received the other two votes.

The most amazing part of all was that everyone agreed that O'Neal would just keep getting better. Even at the end of his rookie season, he was still the youngest player in the NBA. His game was far from perfect. He committed too many fouls against opponents, and his foul shooting was average at best. His jump shot and hook shot also needed improvement.

The best news was this: Shaq was determined to

FACT

As a rookie, O'Neal won many awards, including:

- Rookie of the Year
- NBA All-Star team
- All-rookie team
- NBA Player of the Week (twice)
- All-NBA third team

improve. He wanted to be not just a great player, but the best ever. "I want to dominate," O'Neal liked to say. "And I want to win."[5]

There was one way to get better—keep working. That wasn't difficult for O'Neal. His parents had taught him from the start that hard work was the only way to succeed. The tougher part was getting used to being one of the most famous people in the world. Going up against NBA greats Patrick Ewing and David Robinson was one thing. Going up against a thousand autograph-seeking fans was another.

Chapter 6

Living with Fame

It's not that Shaquille O'Neal wasn't used to attention. He had signed his first autograph at age fifteen. At that time, he was just a high school player in Texas. During his years at Louisiana State, he may have been the most famous college student in America. Beyond that, it's hard for anyone standing seven feet one and weighing over three hundred pounds to blend into a crowd.

But when Shaq hit the NBA, things got crazy. Pro fans were looking for a new superstar, and Shaq seemed to fit the bill. With his big smile, bubbly personality, and thunderous slam dunks, he quickly became the hottest new attraction. Not just in Orlando, but everywhere the team traveled.

It was 2:30 A.M. on a February morning when the visiting Magic walked into the lobby of their Chicago hotel. Outside, it was snowing and 10 degrees. Remember that the Magic were on the home turf of Michael Jordan and the Chicago Bulls. Still, more than two hundred fans stuffed into a hotel lobby in the dead of winter in the middle of the night—just to see O'Neal.

Another night, in Sacramento, so many fans crowded around the Orlando team bus that it couldn't move for an hour. After a while, Shaq tried to disguise himself. He put a floppy, curly black wig over his shaved head and managed to walk right past the fans, who were still staring at the bus on the Shaq Watch.

Shaq always tries to be gracious to fans; his parents taught him to be polite to everyone. But often, he can't sign autographs or pose for pictures without fear of being mobbed for hours.

Does he enjoy being famous?

"It's fun, but sometimes it's difficult," O'Neal said. "I can't go to the mall. I can't go to restaurants. Stuff like that. But that's all right. I can handle it."[1]

Reporters were as interested as fans in the NBA's new sensation. During O'Neal's rookie year, more than one hundred fifty requests came in each week asking for interviews. Shaq couldn't do

Shaq's youth and intensity make him a popular star.

them all. Even so, he averaged twenty to thirty interviews weekly.

O'Neal describes himself as a loner. He obviously likes attention, though. Why else would his vanity license plates read "SHAQ 32" and "HAND-SUM?" Why else would he buy a full-length leather coat with a Superman emblem on the back?

Because O'Neal doesn't cook (microwavable spaghetti and lasagna fill his freezer), his idea of dining is breezing through a fast food drive-thru. Shopping for clothing? The tailor comes to his home. Movies? He sneaks into shows at the last second and sits in the back row.

To get away from it all, Shaq bought a five-thou-sand-square-foot house near Orlando. It sits on a golf course that O'Neal never uses. There isn't much in the house, just a leather couch, a pool table, video games, a bedroom set, and a television. He lives there with Dennis Tracey, who is Shaq's personal assistant. The two men met when Shaq was being recruited by LSU. Tracey walked onto the basketball team after writing coach Dale Brown a letter asking for a tryout. When O'Neal was a freshman, Tracey was a junior. The two quickly became friends.

"Shaq enjoys his private time to himself," Tracey said. "He likes to be alone on game days and when he's not feeling so great. Maybe he's down about the way he's playing or the way the team is playing. He jumps in his car and turns up his music. He just goes for a ride for a couple of hours. He'll come back and be all right."[2]

O'Neal's hobbies are like those of many other young people. He loves amusement parks, is crazy about Nintendo and other video games, adores movies, especially those about martial arts, and he is such a fan of rap music that he put three turntables in his home and spends hours spinning records, pretending he is a disk jockey. As a rookie, he appeared on Arsenio Hall's television show with rapper Fu Schnickens. Later, Shaq cut rap albums of his own.

That's the fun side. There is also a serious side to O'Neal. On Thanksgiving, he pulled seven thousand dollars from his own wallet to feed three hundred fifty people in a homeless shelter in Orlando. Often, he will quietly visit children in hospitals to try to cheer them up.

Perhaps that attitude has a lot to do with Shaq's appeal to young people. In 1993, a survey found him to be the most popular sports star among America's fourth and fifth graders.

Shaq's big personality—and his gigantic smile—have certainly made him popular with

FACT

Some of Shaquille O'Neal's favorite things:

Food: Spaghetti and meatballs, orange soda
Movie: Anything with kung fu
Music: Rap
Hobbies: Jet skis, video games
Athlete: Hakeem Olajuwon
Hero: Phillip Harrison, his father
Vacation: Disney World

advertisers. Even before he joined the NBA, dozens of companies lined up to have him endorse their products. Each was sure he would be a hit, and each wanted Shaq to be the spokesperson for their product.

Soon, Shaq was all over television. In one ad, he was gulping down soda during a pickup game with youngsters. In another, he was jumping into orbit in a company's basketball shoes. He endorsed clothing, trading cards, and action figures.

Some critics thought it was all too much. They wondered out loud whether the quick fame and money would ruin this rising star. O'Neal insisted that would not happen. "Money doesn't make people change," he said. "People make people change. And I'm not going to let that happen."[3]

To help make sure that did not happen, Shaq's dad retired from the military and moved with Shaq's mother to Orlando. They lived in a nearby neighborhood and made a full-time job of looking after their famous son. "You're never too old to take advice from your parents," Shaq said.[4] The home-cooked meals didn't hurt either.

Some nights, Shaq and Mr. Harrison would sit down to watch videos of his games. They weren't there to applaud his highlights. Rather, they looked for flaws in his game. The key was to turn him into an even greater player.

When his rookie season ended, O'Neal's dad and his head coach, Matt Guokas, both suggested that he take a few months to rest up. But resting wasn't in O'Neal's plans. He took three days—three days!—to relax on the beach, and then he was back in action. He cut his first hip-hop album, called *Shaq Diesel*, as well as a video that ran on MTV. The album went platinum, meaning that it sold more than one million copies. On one song from the album, Shaq sang:

"I'm a role model.

"I'm a role figure.

"I ask myself,

"Can I get any bigger?"

The answer was yes. His next venture was in the movies. O'Neal landing a co-starring role in a movie with Nick Nolte. In the film, titled *Blue Chips*, he played a star college basketball player. That certainly qualifies as acting from something that you know.

Between the acting, the music, and his promotional trips for sponsors, O'Neal was stretched pretty thin. Some Orlando fans worried that he was taking his mind off basketball. Not to worry, he insisted.

"I can stay focused on basketball," Shaq said. "I still remember what my real job is. But if a good business opportunity opens up, you have to take advantage of it. There's time for business and time for basketball."[5]

The time for basketball came late in the summer before Shaq's second pro season. He spent two weeks at a camp run by retired coach Pete Newell. The camp was especially designed for big men, the giants on the court. Newell took one look at Shaq and offered this opinion: The twenty-one-year-old youngster combined Patrick Ewing's strength, Hakeem Olajuwon's agility, and David Robinson's shot-blocking ability. Add a few moves to his game, and O'Neal would be among the best ever.[6]

Actually, O'Neal needed something else—a quality team surrounding him.

Luckily for Shaq, the Magic again won the NBA lottery. That meant they again got the top pick of the best players coming out of college. They selected Chris Webber, a big forward from the University of Michigan. Then the Magic turned around and traded Webber to the Golden State Warriors for Anfernee Hardaway of Memphis State College, as well as three future first-round picks.

Hardaway was just what the team needed. As a point guard, he was given the job of setting up plays for Shaq. Plus, as an exciting player who could score points himself, he would take pressure off of Shaq.

David Robinson of the San Antonio Spurs is one of the great shot blockers of the NBA. Here, he's got Shaq covered.

No longer could other teams triple-team the giant in the middle.

O'Neal and Hardaway had played together in All-Star games since they were both in high school. They were close friends and couldn't wait to become teammates.

The Magic made another change before the start of the 1993–94 season. Coach Matt Guokas took a job as the team's vice-president of basketball operations. A new coach, Brian Hill, was hired. Hill immediately changed the Magic's game plan to suit the styles of O'Neal and Hardaway. He put in an up-tempo style of play, in which the Magic would constantly be running.

"I think we have the leadership, maturity and experience to try to take this team to the next level," Hill told reporters. "That's the challenge we face. All of a sudden we're going from an expansion team to a team with great expectations. Our goal is to be a playoff team."[7]

Shaquille O'Neal could not agree more.

Chapter 7

Magic on the Court

From the start of the 1993–94 season, it was clear that the Magic was an improved club. Shaquille O'Neal, in his second season, was getting better each game. He was confident now. There were no more rookie jitters—if that had ever been a problem at all.

The team around O'Neal was also better. Rookie Anfernee Hardaway, who went by the nickname "Penny," moved in as the starting point guard. Hardaway was a magician with the ball. Adding him to the lineup forced other teams to stop triple-teaming O'Neal, and that meant more scoring chances for the big man.

The rest of the squad was also coming together. Forward Nick Anderson helped Shaq fight for the tough rebounds, guard Dennis Scott shot in bombs from three-point range, and veteran Scott Skiles, a six-foot-one spark plug, had the job of bringing the ball up the court. Guiding it all was new coach Brian Hill, who said he planned to build a club that could stay strong for a decade.

"The sky is the limit for this team," Scott said at the start of the season. "The key is the big man. I think Shaquille is enjoying being Shaquille O'Neal right now. He likes the limelight. He's an individual with his own charisma and way with the crowds."[1]

FACT

One way teams evaluate NBA players is by the "Tendex Ratings." The system adds together the player's points, rebounds, assists, and blocks. Then, turnovers and missed shots are subtracted. The total is divided by a player's minutes played. The standings for the 1993–94 season:

Player	Rating
1. Shaquille O'Neal, Orlando	84.1
2. David Robinson, San Antonio	83.9
3. Hakeem Olajuwon, Houston	80.1
4. Shawn Kemp, Seattle	75.2
5. Charles Barkley, Phoenix	73.8

The mix of players worked well. Orlando won 50 games and lost just 32. O'Neal continued to grow as a top NBA center. He finished second in the NBA in scoring (29.3 points per game), and second in rebounding (13.2 per game).

Especially exciting was the combo of Shaq and Penny. Each night, it seemed, the two young players would be on the television highlights. One night, against the Atlanta Hawks, Hardaway dribbled up court, did a full-circle turn while dribbling, and threw an alley-oop pass that O'Neal stuffed through the net. Moments later, Shaq returned the favor. He drew tough coverage under the net, so he flipped a blind pass behind his back. Hardaway caught the pass and threw up a three-point attempt: Swish.

"Some nights I feel like Penny and I are inside each other's brains," Shaq said after the game. "It's like I know what he's going to do before he does it. Maybe that's why our team is called the Magic."[2]

For the first time in its history, Orlando made the NBA playoffs in 1993–94. Unfortunately for Magic fans, the post-season stay was short. In the first round, the team became the Indiana Pacers' first-ever playoff victim. Making things worse, the Pacers won it in three straight games. After fifty regular-season wins, the Magic could manage none in the post-season.

Shaq knew he had to take some blame for the collapse. Many fans thought he was outplayed by Indiana center Rik Smits, a seven-foot-four bean pole who had never been considered a star. In the series, Shaq missed more than half of his free throws. He was embarrassed, and he promised to improve.

That summer, Shaq didn't make any movies or cut any new rap albums. Instead, he joined the United States national team—Dream Team II—for the World Championships in Toronto. His performance settled a number of issues, including his devotion to the sport. Shaq was far and away the best player on the court. He was the only player that foreign teams had no answer for.

One game, against Russia, was too close for comfort. Shaq, who had a sore back, was on the bench. With seventeen minutes left, the Russians were within seven points. The U.S. sharp-shooters were struggling. It seemed that the Americans might be ripe for an upset.

Then O'Neal reentered the game. He scored eleven points in a three-minute span. He slammed, jammed, dribbled, and stuffed. The Americans cruised to an easy victory. "We had a plan to stop O'Neal," Russian coach Sergei Belov said afterward. "But we didn't have the players to execute the plan."[3]

Shaq missed more than half of his free throws in the
playoff series against the Indiana Pacers.

After the World Championship Tournament, Shaq hired private coach Buzz Braman to help him work on foul shooting. Braman, nicknamed the "Shot Doctor," taught Shaq to relax more before each attempt and to picture the ball going through the net before he even threw it. Shaq also went to work out at a big man's summer camp run by Pete Newell, an old college coach. There, he practiced his foot work and spin moves in the hot sun. It was hard work, but Shaq never shied from hard work.

O'Neal knew that it wasn't points that counted, and it wasn't All-Star games. It was championships that separated the great players from the very good ones. Shaq wanted to be considered great.

"He's going to need to win a title," former Boston Celtics coach Tom Heinsohn said of O'Neal. "Until he wins that, they'll be saying he can't carry a team. He wasn't ready before, but he's getting the skills now. He's worked hard on the skills."[4]

O'Neal's college team in Louisiana had never gone far in the NCAA Tournament. His first try in the NBA playoffs was disappointing. So he promised himself that in 1994–95 the Magic would go further.

That would not be easy. The NBA boasted many talented teams. First and foremost were the Houston Rockets, the defending champions. They were

Shaq goes over the top of Hakeem Olajuwon.

led by Hakeem "The Dream" Olajuwon. Shaq had always considered Olajuwon as something of a role model for the classy way he carried himself on and off the basketball court.

Then there were the New York Knicks, Orlando's main rival in the NBA's Atlantic Division. The Knicks were a tough team that had lost to Houston in the 1994 NBA Finals. Their center,

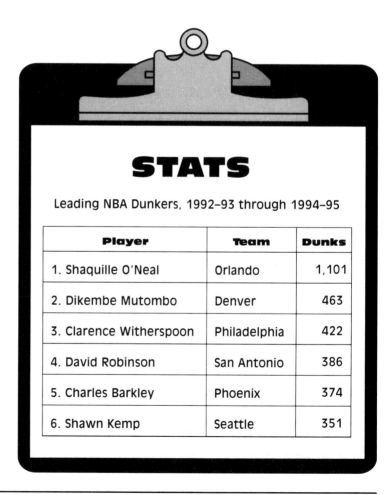

STATS

Leading NBA Dunkers, 1992–93 through 1994–95

Player	Team	Dunks
1. Shaquille O'Neal	Orlando	1,101
2. Dikembe Mutombo	Denver	463
3. Clarence Witherspoon	Philadelphia	422
4. David Robinson	San Antonio	386
5. Charles Barkley	Phoenix	374
6. Shawn Kemp	Seattle	351

Patrick Ewing, was a cagey veteran. He always gave O'Neal trouble with his quick moves.

The San Antonio Spurs would also be a factor. Their center, David Robinson, had been O'Neal's hero when Shaq was a high school star. But in the NBA they were bitter rivals who exchanged nasty words and an occasional push or shove.

The Chicago Bulls would also be contenders. Midway through the season, Bulls superstar Michael Jordan came out of an eighteen-month retirement. His return lifted the team and made it a threat to go all the way.

And what was Orlando? A young team, for sure, led by two players—O'Neal and Hardaway—who had not yet even reached their twenty-third birthdays. How could such an inexperienced club be expected to compete against the league's cagey veterans? Talent, that's how. In his third season, Shaq just kept improving—in shooting, rebounding, even passing. He and Hardaway continued their game of getting into each other's minds.

Between them, the two men averaged 50 points per game. Dennis Scott and Nick Anderson also chipped in.

Also, the Magic added Horace Grant to the mix in 1994. Grant had been a teammate of Jordan's in Chicago, where the Bulls won three NBA titles. He knew how to win. He knew how to help a club by scoring and rebounding, and he took the defensive pressure off of Shaq, allowing the young center to concentrate even more on scoring.

The Magic breezed through the NBA's Atlantic Division in 1994–95. They won 57 games and lost just 25. That record put them two games ahead of the New York Knicks, who had won the division the year before. In front of the friendly crowds at the

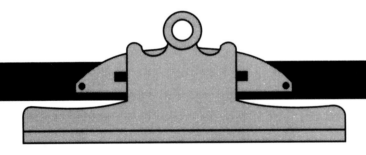

STATS

Here is how O'Neal compares with the other NBA centers:

Player	Points per game	Rebounds per game	Blocks per game
Patrick Ewing	20.5	8.6	2.5
Hakeem Olajuwon	22.4	11.6	3.1
Shaquille O'Neal	27.3	12.8	3.0
David Robinson	24.7	12.5	4.1

Orlando Arena, the Magic won an incredible 39 of their 41 games.

O'Neal's numbers were terrific, too. He led the entire league by scoring an average of 29.3 points per game. He was second in the NBA in shooting percentage, third in rebounds, and sixth in blocked shots. He scored 40 or more points in nine games and 30 or more in an incredible thirty-eight games.

Not surprisingly, Shaq was voted the starting center for the NBA's Eastern Conference in the 1995 All-Star Game. With Magic teammate Hardaway to get him the ball, O'Neal made 9 of 16 shots. He finished with 26 points and 7 rebounds. Despite his effort, the East lost the game, 139–112.

By the mid-90s, Shaq had developed a tough rival. He and Alonzo Mourning, the center for the Charlotte Hornets, seemed to have great games each time they faced each other. Mourning was the second pick of the NBA draft in 1992—the year that Shaq was picked first. The matchup of these two great young players reminded longtime NBA fans of the classic battles between Wilt Chamberlain and Bill Russell, or Larry Bird and Magic Johnson.

"Shaq is an alligator," Mourning once told reporters. "And it's challenging to wrestle alligators one-on-one. You have to fight fire with fire. If not, you're fighting a losing battle."[5]

Patrick Ewing watches in awe as Shaq slams one in.

Shaq's view of the rivalry was a bit friendlier. "When you see two big guys on the court making faces at each other, you think they don't like each other," he said. "But that's how it is supposed to be in a competitive situation. Off the court we're cool."[6]

Typical of the O'Neal-Mourning duels was a sweat-drenched beauty in January 1995. The two centers occupied center stage in a game that had the mood of a heavyweight championship bout.

Halfway through the contest, Orlando was down, 50–46. Then O'Neal scored on a jump hook.

FACT

The season before O'Neal landed in Orlando, the Magic had the second-worst record in the NBA. Here is a look at the team before Shaq, and its improvement during his first three seasons:

Season	W	L	Finish
1991–92	21	61	Seventh
1992–93	41	41	Fourth
1993–94	50	32	Second
1994–95	57	25	First

Then he muscled in a bucket and converted a three-point play. Then Grant passed to O'Neal, who passed back to Grant for a hoop. Suddenly, Orlando led, 53–50, and never gave back the lead.

At game's end, the two stars had almost identical numbers. O'Neal finished with 35 points and 15 rebounds, Mourning had 33 points and 12 rebounds. More importantly, the Magic beat the Hornets, 109–98.

The Magic's regular-season finish in 1994–95 pleased the team and Coach Hill, but Shaq had bigger ideas. He remembered the playoff embarrassment of the year before, and he did not want to lose in the first round again. Shaq told no one, but this season, his goal was to get to the NBA finals.

Chapter 8

Taking It to the Top

Ask Shaquille O'Neal to name his heroes in sports, and he'll give you Joe Montana, Wayne Gretzky, and Kareem Abdul-Jabbar. They're great names, superstar players, and all-around good guys.

The three have something else in common. Montana won four NFL Super Bowls as quarterback for the San Francisco 49ers. Gretzky won four NHL Stanley Cups with the Edmonton Oilers. Abdul-Jabbar won seven NBA titles with the Milwaukee Bucks and Los Angeles Lakers.

O'Neal wants to join that select crew. He wants to be both a great player and a title winner. He wants championship rings for each of his fingers.

In the 1995 NBA playoffs, he began working toward that goal.

When the post-season began, more was expected from the Orlando Magic. The team had been eliminated quickly the season before, losing three straight to the Indiana Pacers. A lot of folks chalked that up to inexperience. It was, after all, the first time most of the team's players had been in the playoffs. But now they were back and there were no excuses. A team that wins its division can't claim to be an underdog.

To win the NBA title, the Magic would have to win four playoff rounds. That was quite a challenge, but O'Neal was more than ready. The day before the post-season started, he told reporters, "I'm so excited right now, I can't wait. I feel like it's Christmas Eve. I can't wait for tomorrow to come. Believe me, I'll be ready."[1]

He sure was. In the first round, the Magic breezed past the Boston Celtics, three games to one. The Celtics, to be true, were not a very good team. To make up for their lack of talent, they played a rough style that Orlando coach Brian Hill dubbed "Hack-a-Shaq."[2] In other words, nearly every time O'Neal got the ball, the Celtics simply fouled him. They tried to push him away from the basket. If he couldn't dunk, they figured, he'd have a tough time scoring.

Of course, the strategy meant that Shaq kept

going to the foul line. In one contest, O'Neal was able to nail 13 out of 20 free-throw attempts. When Boston center Eric Montross fouled out, Shaq moved in for easy jams and rebounds. Even though free throws are the weakest part of Shaq's game, he made enough for the Magic to win easily.

Next up were the Chicago Bulls, led by Michael Jordan. A few months earlier, Jordan came back from his eighteen-month retirement, during which he tried playing pro baseball. With Jordan back, the Bulls were considered a good bet to return to the level that won them championships for three straight years.

Air Jordan vs. Shaq was billed as the ultimate basketball battle. In truth, they usually played on different areas of the court—O'Neal inside, Jordan outside. Only occasionally would Jordan soar down the lane to find Shaq blocking the path with his giant arms spread like wings.

Mostly, Shaq lined up against Chicago's three centers—Luc Longley, Will Perdue, and Bill Wennington. Borrowing their plan from the Celtics, the trio pushed and shoved Shaq every time he touched the ball. Shaq compared the tough treatment to professional wrestling. "I feel like I'm in a steel cage match and three guys are beating me up," he said after the Bulls won Game Four to tie the series.

STATS

Shaquille O'Neal's
one-game highs:

Field goals: 22
Free throws:15
Rebounds: 28
Assists: 6
Points: 53

Putting out a call for help to his favorite wrestler, Shaq said, "Hulk Hogan, I need you man."[3]

The next night, the Hulkster showed up. As it turned out, Shaq didn't need any help from the wrestler. Fair and square, he and his teammates won the next two games to take the series.

After Game Six, Jordan and O'Neal hugged on the floor. Jordan told Shaq that, from now on, he was "the man." From now on, it was O'Neal's job to dominate the NBA.

Maybe so, but it wasn't getting any easier. In the next playoff round—the NBA semi-finals—the Magic faced the Indiana Pacers. This was the team that had humiliated Orlando in the playoffs a year earlier. The Pacers were a talented team that had won the league's Central Division in 1994–95. They were led by Reggie Miller—a fast-talking, smooth-shooting guard. Their seven-foot-four center, Rik Smits, had been the best in the league at stopping Shaq.

This time, Shaq promised, things would be different, and he began working to prove it. Before Game One of the series, he exercised in the Magic's workout room. He lifted a stack of weights so forcefully that he ripped the cord holding the weights together. He went to a tattoo parlor and got the words "The world is mine" printed on his shoulder for all to see. He showed up for the series with fire in his eyes.

Shaq dominated. He averaged 31 points per game in the series. The Pacers were no pushover and the series went seven games, but there was no doubt which was the better team and who was the best player.

The most memorable play came in Game Five, which the Magic won. It came late in the second quarter with the Magic up by eight. The ball came loose at midcourt and a half-dozen players raced to grab it.

Shaq got there first. He knocked the ball with his right hand, breezing past Indiana guard Byron Scott and breaking into the open court. His plan was never in question. As O'Neal drove to the basket, Reggie Miller wrapped his toothpick arms around Shaq's three-hundred-pound body and held on for dear life.

Shaq broke through Miller's arms, rose to the rim as the whistle shrieked, and completed a rim-rattling dunk. Upon landing, he let out a scream of relief, then toppled over a cameraman sitting on the out-of-bounds line. Smiling, O'Neal carefully lifted his victim from the court and dusted him off. He had already dusted off the Pacers.

O'Neal had succeeded in reaching his first goal.

Orlando was in the 1995 NBA Finals. Now, if the team could only win, things would be that much sweeter.

The Magic's opponent for the title were the Houston Rockets. The Rockets were the defending champions. Their center, Hakeem "The Dream" Olajuwon, had been the NBA's Most Valuable Player the season before. Olajuwon played a very different style from O'Neal. On the court, Olajuwon is a blur of moves, a shooting guard in a seven-foot body. O'Neal simply is a bull, three hundred pounds of fury.

Olajuwon, at thirty-two, brought experience to the title fight. O'Neal, at twenty-three, brought youthful enthusiasm. One thing the two men had in common was mutual respect.

"He can do it all," Shaq said of Olajuwon. "He can go outside, inside. Go left, go right. He can dribble. He's the perfect all-around big-man player. And he doesn't cry, he just plays basketball. Off the court, he's a class act, soft-spoken, handsome. Like me."[4]

Olajuwon returned the kind words. "Oh, Shaq is such a force inside," he said. "The best way for me to play him is to step up my game. I don't know if I'm happy about going up against Shaq."[5]

As it turned out, Olajuwon had every reason to

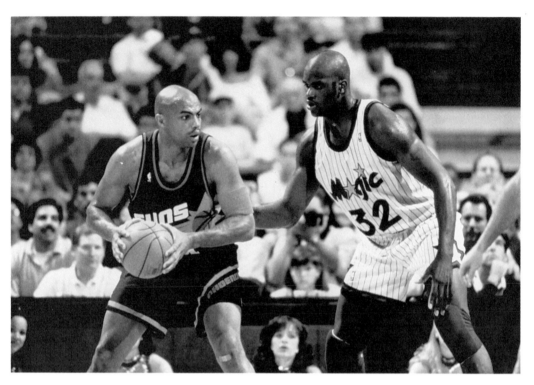

O'Neal covers Charles Barkley of the Phoenix Suns. Shaq excels at both defense and offense.

be happy. In this case, at least, experience won out. The middle belonged to Shaquille O'Neal through much of the championship series, but Hakeem Olajuwon was the one left standing at the end.

The Rockets won the series in four straight games. Shaq held up his end, averaging 27 points per game, but Olajuwon played even better. He averaged 32 points per game, and he used his experience and quick moves to beat the younger man.

Getting swept in the finals was a humbling experience, but Shaq has nothing to be ashamed of. In three short seasons, he had led the Magic from being an NBA doormat to its second-best team. He has worked hard to improve his game, spending hours shooting foul shots in an otherwise empty gym.

Sometime, perhaps soon, the tables will turn. Shaq will reach the point where he can dominate Olajuwon, as well as every other NBA center. Indeed, there seems no question that O'Neal will be basketball's most important player for years to come. Consider this: Olajuwon led the Rockets to the NBA title at age thirty-two. Shaq won't reach that age until the year 2004. Imagine how much better he might be by then.

Shaq's goal is to cover his fingers with championship rings. That could take years, but Shaq says

The Houston Rockets play catch-up as Shaq slams the
ball through the hoop.

STATS

If Shaquille O'Neal retires before he wins a title, he would not be the only great basketball player to finish his pro career without a championship. Here's a list of Hall of Fame players who never played on a championship team:

Players	Years in the NBA	Career points per game
Elgin Baylor	14	27.4
Walt Bellamy	14	20.1
Bob Lanier	14	20.1
Nate Thurmond	14	15.0
Calvin Murphy	13	17.9
Dave Bing	12	20.3

he plans to have a long career. Sometimes, teammates catch him staring at the NBA record book. He is looking for records he might break some day. The one that interests him most—twenty-one seasons in the league, a mark shared by Kareem Abdul-Jabbar and Moses Malone.

There is a desire burning in the heart of this young man. He wants to be the best at whatever he tries—business, charity, rapping, or basketball. It doesn't really matter which he's doing, Shaq puts his all into each of them. Anything less than total effort is a waste of time, he says.

That is a value his parents instilled in him as a young boy. "Give it your all," his dad used to say. "Anything less and you're just cheating yourself."[6]

Coach Dale Brown taught the same lessons at Louisiana State University. And in the NBA, superstars like Michael Jordan and Hakeem Olajuwon showed Shaq that the only way to become a champion is to have the heart of a champion.

There is no question that O'Neal has the heart. The championships ought to follow.

Chapter Notes

Chapter 1

1. John Smallwood, "That's Awe, Folks; Magic Stars Learn to Treat Jordan as Mortal," *Philadelphia Daily News*, May 18, 1995, p. 79.

2. Ibid.

3. Phil Long, "Shaq at the Top of the Heap," *Miami Herald*, June 6, 1995, p. D1.

4. Terry Pluto, "Through It All, Shaq Stands Tall—Even With a Bad Back," *Akron Beacon Journal*, August 9, 1994, p. D7.

5. Kenneth Shouler, "Slamming His Point Home," *Inside Sports Magazine*, June 1995, p. 62

6. Diane Pucin, "Shaq a Fortress Towering Over Game," *Philadelphia Inquirer*, November 21, 1991, p. BB12.

Chapter 2

1. Ira Berkow, "Shaq's Rap Has Message for the '90s," *Lexington Herald-Leader*, November 2, 1994, p. C1

2. Ibid.

3. Shaquille O'Neal and Jack McCallum, *Shaq Attack!* (New York: Hyperion Press, 1993), p. 19.

4. Jerry Tipton, "Cats Must Post Up on a Bigger, Better Shaquille," *Lexington Herald-Leader,* January 4, 1991, p. B1.

5. Dick Weiss, "Shaq Attack Frightening in Its Size," *Philadelphia Daily News,* February 12, 1991, p. 77.

6. Ibid.

7. Ernie Trubiano, "USC's Raines Signs Stratford Standouts," *The State of Columbia, S.C.,* May 27, 1989, p. 5C.

Chapter 3

1. David Brumner, "Brown Takes Blame for Loss to Kansas," *Wichita Eagle,* November 23, 1989, p. 8C.

2. Jerry Tipton, "Coaches See LSU Atop SEC," *Lexington Herald-Leader,* November 2, 1989, p. C1.

3. Austin Wilson, "LSU'S O'Neal Growing into a Force in Middle," *Lexington Herald-Leader,* February 16, 1990, p. D4.

4. David Moore, "Shaq O'Neal: The Coming of the Next Wilt," *1993 Complete Handbook of Pro Basketball,* (New York: Dutton, 1993) p. 30.

5. Chuck Schoffner, "NBA Can Hold for This Tiger," *Charlotte Observer,* July 10, 1990, p. 2C.

6. Associated Press, "LSU's O'Neal Sets Record

With 53 Points," *Lexington Herald-Leader,* December 20, 1990, p. D1.

7. Schoffner, p. 2C.

Chapter 4

1. Dick Weiss, "Shaquille O'Neal Becomes a Big Wheel," *Philadelphia Daily News,* February 12, 1991, p. 77.

2. Diane Pucin, "Shaq a Fortress Towering Over Game," *Philadelphia Inquirer,* November 21, 1991, p. BB12.

3. David Newton, "Shackled? LSU Star O'Neal Poses Problems for Gamecocks," *The State of Columbia, S.C.,* February 19, 1992, p. 1C.

4. Weiss, p. 77.

5. Andre Christopher, "LSU Falls; O'Neal Urged to Turn Pro," *Miami Herald,* March 15, 1992, p. 6D.

6. Ray Richardson, "O'Neal's News Excites Timberwolves," *St. Paul Pioneer Press,* April 4, 1992, p. 1B.

7. Pucin, p. BB12.

Chapter 5

1. Mary Schmitt, "Shaquille's Level of Superstardom Grows by Magic," *St. Paul Pioneer Press,* October 22, 1992, p. 1C.

2. Johnette Howard, "Shaq Attack Magical

Moves, Size and Strength Are Creating an NBA Sensation," *Detroit Free Press,* November 17, 1992, p. 1D.

3. Ibid.

4. Associated Press, "Chamberlain Wilts at Shaq Comparisons," *St. Paul Pioneer Press,* December 20, 1992, p. 8B.

5. Howard, p. 1D.

Chapter 6

1. Kelly Carter, "Fame a Burden? Not for Shaq," *Orange County Register,* February 2, 1993, p. 1C.

2. Shaun Powell, "Coming Out Party," *Miami Herald,* October 16, 1992, p. 1D.

3. Terry Pluto, "A League of His Own," *Akron Beacon Journal,* January 28, 1993, p. B1.

4. Ibid.

5. Fred Goodall, "Shaq Proud of His Summer Vacation," *St. Paul Pioneer Press,* October 31, 1993, p. 1C.

6. Michael Holley, "O'Neal Is Seizing Moment," *Akron Beacon Journal,* December 4, 1993, p. B1.

7. Goodall, p. 1C.

Chapter 7

1. Goodall, "Shaq Proud of His Summer Vacation," *St. Paul Pioneer Press,* October 31, 1993, p. 1C.

2. Michael Holley, "O'Neal Is Seizing Moment," *Akron Beacon Journal,* December 4, 1993, p. B1.

3. Kenneth Shouler, "Slamming His Point Home," *Inside Sports Magazine,* June 1995, p. 62.

4. Ibid.

5. Scott Fowler, "Mourning's Back and So Is Shaq," *Charlotte Observer,* November 9, 1994, p. 1B.

6. Ibid.

Chapter 8

1. Tim Povtak, "O'Neal Licking His Chops," *Orlando Sentinel,* May 28, 1995, p. 1D.

2. Ira Winderman, "Shaq Hacked, Fights Back," *Fort Lauderdale Sun-Sentinel,* May 24, 1995, p. C1.

3. Phil Taylor, "Hoopla," *Sports Illustrated,* May 22, 1995, p. 24.

4. Frank Lawlor, "The Finals Center on These Two Dissimilar Stars," *Philadelphia Inquirer,* June 7, 1995, p. D1.

5. Ira Winderman, "O'Neal, Hakeem: Esteem," *Charlotte Observer,* June 7, 1995, p. 1B.

6. Weiss, "Shaq Attack Frightening in Its Size," *Philadelphia Daily News,* February 12, 1991, p. 77.

Career Statistics

College

Team	Year	G	FG%	REB	AST	PTS	AVG
LSU	89–90	32	.573	385	61	445	13.9
LSU	90–91	28	.628	411	45	774	27.6
LSU	91–92	30	.615	421	46	722	24.1
Totals		90	.610	1,217	152	1,941	21.6

NBA

Team	Year	G	FG%	REB	AST	STL	BLK	PTS	AVG
Magic	92–93	81	.562	1,122	152	60	286	1,893	23.4
Magic	93–94	81	.599	1,072	195	76	231	2,377	29.3
Magic	94–95	79	.583	901	214	73	192	2,315	29.3
Totals		241	.583	3,095	561	209	709	6,585	27.3

G=Games Played

FG%=Field Goal Percentage

REB=Rebounds

AST=Assists

STL=Steals

BLK=Blocks

PTS=Points

AVG=Points Per Game Average

Where to Write
Shaquille O'Neal

Mr. Shaquille O'Neal
c/o Orlando Magic
1 Magic Place
Orlando, FL 32801

Index